W9-BNY-835

Erosion

Erosion

Joshua Rutten

THE CHILD'S WORLD®, INC.

Library of Congress Cataloging-in-Publication Data
Rutten, Joshua.
Erosion / by Joshua Rutten.
p.   cm.
Includes index.
Summary: Questions and answers introduce
the basics of erosion, its causes, effects,
and possible solutions for slowing down the process.
ISBN 1-56766-508-X (smythe-sewn library reinforced : alk. paper)
1. Erosion—Miscellanea—Juvenile literature.
[1. Erosion—Miscellanea. 2. Questions and answers.]   I. Title.
QE571.R88   1998
551.3'02—dc21   97-34542
CIP
AC

Photo Credits

© 1995 DPA/Dembinsky Photo Assoc. Inc: 16
© Adam Jones/Dembinsky Photo Assoc. Inc: 6, 23
© David Austen/Tony Stone Images: 19
© Dugald Bremner/Tony Stone Images: 13
© Gary Braasch/Tony Stone Images: 20
© Jacques Janquox/Tony Stone Worldwide: cover
© James Randklev/Tony Stone Images: 26
© Kay Shaw: 24
© Keith Wood/Tony Stone Images: 15
© Lori Adamski Peek/Tony Stone Images: 29
© 1997 Mark E. Gibson/Dembinsky Photo Assoc. Inc: 30
© Ric Ergenbright/Tony Stone Images: 2
© Steve Taylor/Tony Stone Images: 10
© TSW Agricultural File/Tony Stone Images: 9

On the cover...

Front cover: Erosion by water caused this hillside in Guatemala to wash away.
Page 2: These rocks along an Oregon beach are being shaped by water erosion.

Table of Contents

Earth is a wonderful place. Everywhere you look, you can see strange and beautiful things. Earth is also, however, a place that needs to be cared for. When people think about protecting the world, they often think of saving plants or animals. But what about saving the soil? The loss of soil is called **erosion**. Erosion is a very serious problem.

⇐ Wind and water have changed the shape of this field.

What Is Soil?

When the planet Earth was forming, there wasn't any soil. Mountains, rocks, and water were the only things to be found. Over thousands of years, wind and water broke the rocks into sand and dust. Then plants began to grow in this dirt. Very slowly, animals began to live on Earth and eat the plants.

When a plant or animal died, it **decayed**, or broke down into tiny pieces. Over time, the tiny pieces were mixed with the broken rocks. This mixture is what makes up soil.

Soil like this is made up of rocks and decayed plants and animals. ⇒

Soil is very important. Without soil, many of Earth's creatures would not be able to stay alive. That is because soil is at the beginning of many **food chains**. In a food chain, plants and animals depend on other plants and animals to stay alive.

Without soil, plants would not be able to survive. And without plants, many plant-eating animals would die. The world would be a very different place if there were no soil!

⇐ This sunflower plant is just beginning to grow in the rich soil.   11

Can Water Cause Erosion?

Erosion can be caused by many things. One form of erosion is caused by moving water. When water flows in a line, it forms a path, or a **channel**. As it moves along the channel, the water carries loose dirt along with it. This is called *channel erosion*.

This stream has changed the nearby rocks through channel erosion. ⇒

Rivers move a lot of soil through channel erosion. But when the soil reaches the end of a river, it stops moving. It sinks to the bottom and piles up. This pile of dirt is called a **delta**. Big, fast rivers can create huge deltas. The *Mississippi River* delta gets so much soil, it grows 300 feet longer each year!

The Mississippi River delta stretches as far as the eye can see. ⇒

Can Wind Cause Erosion?

Wind can cause erosion, too. As it blows, the wind picks up small, dry pieces of soil. If the wind is strong enough, it can carry soil for hundreds of miles. Sometimes the wind brings lots of dirt and dust to an area. Other times, it blows all of the soil away, leaving the land bare and empty.

⟸ Dust storms like this one carry dirt and dust to other areas.

Can People Cause Erosion?

Plants and trees protect the land from erosion. Their roots hold the soil in place and keep water from washing it away. Plants also protect the ground from strong winds. But people often cut down plants and trees so they can farm or build houses and roads. They do not think about protecting the soil. In these areas, erosion happens quickly. Without the protection of the plants and trees, the rain and wind carry much of the soil away.

This tree's roots can no longer protect the soil from water erosion. ⇒

What Damage Can Erosion Do?

Erosion causes a lot of damage. Many farm areas have been destroyed because the fertile soil has been blown or washed away. Erosion can destroy hillsides, too. When too much rain falls on an eroded hillside, huge parts of the hill can come sliding down. This landslide can destroy homes, block roads, and even hurt people.

But not all erosion damage happens when soil is taken away. Sometimes wind and water move too much dirt to an area. Too much dirt can plug up a river and stop the moving water. This causes floods that can destroy thousands of homes. The floods can also carry the river's fish into areas where they cannot survive.

Floods in Indiana have ruined this small town. ⇒

Can We Learn from Erosion?

Not very long ago, much of the small country of Haiti was covered with forest. But more and more people moved onto the little island. They cut down trees and destroyed the plants.

Today, much of Haiti's soil has been washed into the ocean. Now there is too much dirt in the ocean near Haiti, so some sea plants and fish are dying. And there are areas on the land that will never be able to grow crops again!

What has happened to Haiti could happen anywhere in the world. We should learn from Haiti and protect our land, because we need our farmland for growing food.

⇐ Much like the beaches in Haiti, this beach in Georgia is eroding.

Can We Stop Erosion?

People cannot stop erosion completely. It has been around since the Earth formed, and it is very important. It is nature's way of tearing down old lands and building new ones.

But we can stop the land from eroding too quickly. By planting trees and saving plants, we can help save the soil from the wind and water.

These children are planting a tree near their school. ⇒

Slowly, many people are learning ways to protect the soil. Many farmers plant long lines of trees, called **windbreaks**, near their crops. These trees stop the wind and keep it from blowing away the soil. Other people grow grass and trees in their yards to protect the soil around their homes. If we all work together, erosion will no longer be a problem, and Earth will be a beautiful place for a very long time.

Glossary

channel (CHA–null)
When water flows along a line, it carves a deep path called a channel. A river follows a large channel.

decay (dee–KAY)
When something decays, it breaks down into tiny pieces. Plants and animals decay when they die.

delta (DELL–tuh)
A delta is a pile of soil at the end of a river. Deltas can be big or small.

erosion (ee–ROW–zhun)
Erosion happens when soil is washed away by water or blown away by wind.

food chain (FOOD CHANE)
In a food chain, bigger animals depend on smaller animals and plants for food. Soil is at the beginning of most food chains.

windbreaks (WIND-brakes)
A windbreak is a long line of trees that stops the wind. Farmers plant windbreaks to keep the soil from blowing away.

Index